In His Steps

By

Dennis B. Harris

Edited by Kay Harris

Illustrated by Lee Herring

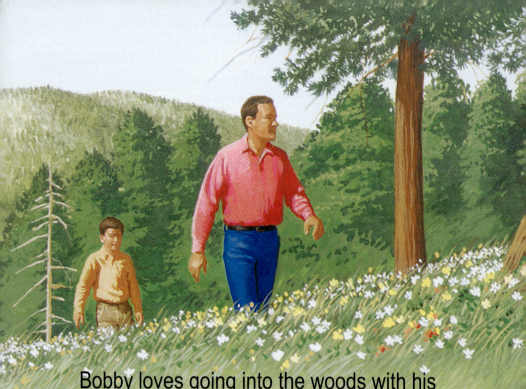

Bobby loves going into the woods with his dad. It is a special time that they have together. They talk about all kinds of stuff, school and friends. They tell each other funny stories and jokes. Sometimes, Bobby's dad tells him things that are grown-up and serious.

They had been in this part of the woods before. Bobby had always loved the smell of the leaves. The mountain had a smell all its own. The Spring air was crisp and the flowers, grass and leaves were fresh and beautiful.

Bobby is 8 years old now. His dad has been taking him into these woods for three years. He expected his dad to take the same trail they had always taken. But, today he started up the side of the mountain instead of going along the stream in the bottom.

Almost immediately, the trail got narrow and steep. But his dad was going slow and the climb wasn't too bad. Bobby was looking at the ground and stepping in his dad's tracks. It was fun to try and walk in his footsteps.

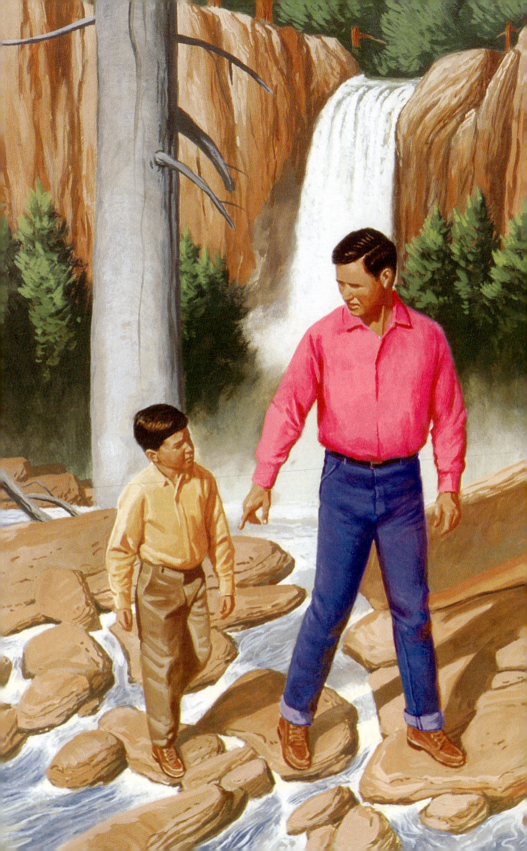

As they climbed a bit further, the trail was above the trees at the bottom of the hill. Bobby's dad stopped and said, "Did you see that beautiful bird in the tree?" Bobby looked where his dad was pointing, but the bird had already flown away.

They walked on and his dad stopped again and said, "Did you see that rabbit?" When Bobby looked it was gone.

Some of the branches from the brush and the smaller trees grew very close to the trail. They would have hit Bobby in the face if his dad hadn't been holding the branches so that Bobby could go under them.

The trail went past a small waterfall. As his dad crossed the stream, he tried to point out to Bobby the beautiful trout that he saw in the pool at the bottom. Bobby was so busy trying to put his little feet in the bootprints from his dad that he missed the trout. But he didn't miss the footprints!

On they went. Soon, Bobby was almost able to walk exactly where his dad's bootprint was. Once, he followed so closely that he accidentally stepped on the back of his dad's big boot. Mostly, he was trying so hard to walk where his dad had walked, that his dad had to stop and wait for him to catch up.

Bam!!! A branch hit Bobby in the face. It didn't hurt, but it sure did surprise him. His dad had been holding the branches up, but now, his dad was too far ahead of him to help with the branches. Bobby had to run to catch up. First, he had to crawl over a tree that had fallen in the trail. It was hard to do. By the time he had gotten over it, his dad was even farther away. "Dad, wait for me," he yelled. His dad patiently stopped

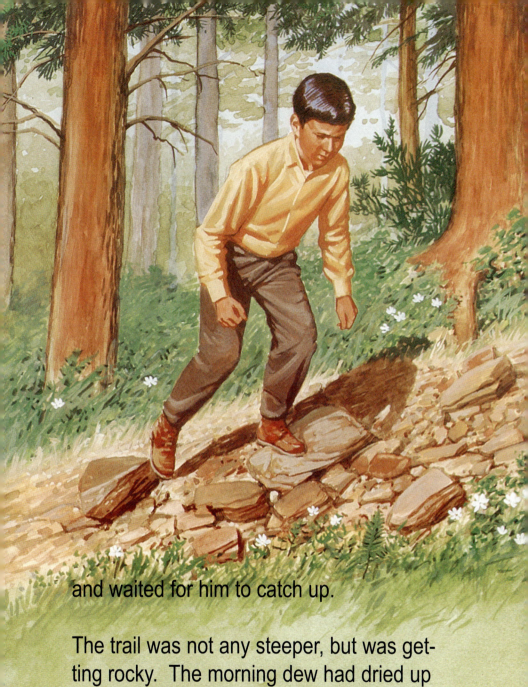

and waited for him to catch up.

The trail was not any steeper, but was getting rocky. The morning dew had dried up and the footprints were harder to see. Bobby had to look really hard to see them. Then... they vanished completely...

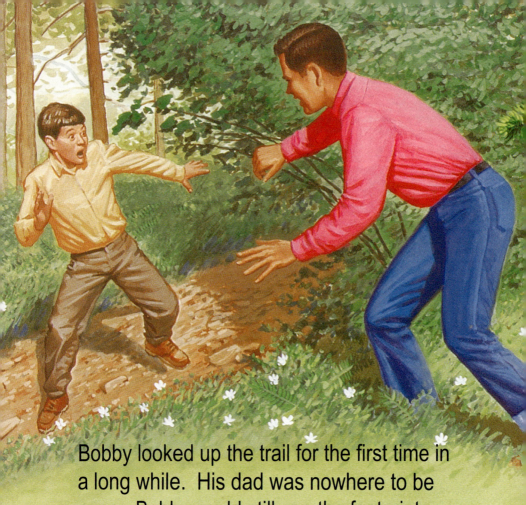

Bobby looked up the trail for the first time in a long while. His dad was nowhere to be seen. Bobby could still see the footprints, but where was Dad?

Bobby began to run... and yell... "Dad!"

"Here I am, Bobby," his dad said. He was so close that it scared Bobby. While his dad had been waiting for Bobby to catch up, he had played a trick on him and had stepped off the trail.

It was time for lunch. His dad found a quiet place by the side of the trail. They sat on rocks and ate sandwiches and drank some cool water from the stream that ran by the trail. It was the first time that they had been able to talk together that day. Bobby had been so busy trying to trace his dad's steps that he kept getting too far behind to talk or see the things that his dad wanted to talk about. He hadn't seen the bird or the squirrel. He had not seen the two deer, but he did see their white tails as they ran off. He missed the trout and the flowers growing out of the rock.

He did not miss the branches, however.

Bobby was surprised. It was the first time that he noticed the little stream that ran down alongside the trail. The water was cool and clean.

He began to look around. He could see forever, almost. He did not realize how high they had climbed. It was so beautiful... he could almost touch the clouds, it seemed.

As they began to hike again, Bobby was determined to stay up with his dad. He walked alongside him. His dad held the branches away from his face and they talked about all kinds of things.

They talked about school and church. They talked about the love God has for us and about Jesus.

They planned a vacation to the ocean this summer.

Bobby's dad explained how sick his grandfather was and that he might be going to Heaven soon. They shared a lot of things as they walked along together.

Bobby didn't notice that the bootprints were now behind them. But, he did notice the beautiful eagle and the deer grazing in the meadow.

His dad didn't have to point out the squirrel on the rock by the trail or the nest with the bird eggs. Bobby saw them first, in fact.

Hiking was so much fun.

Soon, Bobby decided to walk in front of his dad so he could lead the way. The trail was easy to see and the climb wasn't very steep. Ahead, Bobby could see low hanging branches and was able to walk under them. He was the leader, now.

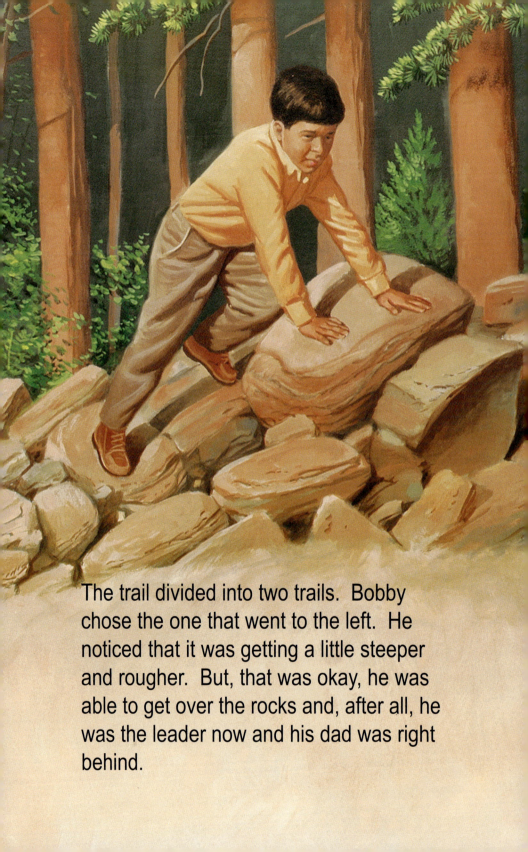

The trail divided into two trails. Bobby chose the one that went to the left. He noticed that it was getting a little steeper and rougher. But, that was okay, he was able to get over the rocks and, after all, he was the leader now and his dad was right behind.

The air was cooler and so crisp. Everything was quiet and still. Not like the city, where the cars and factories were noisy. It was almost too quiet.

Suddenly, he was looking straight down. WOW!!! He had not even see the edge!

He looked back and... HEY! WHERE WAS DAD?!!! He was no where to be seen. Also, where is the trail?!! "DAD! DAD!" yelled Bobby.

He headed down the way he had come up. What he thought had been the trail was almost too steep to run without falling down. He ran, anyway, over the rocks he jumped, under the branches... "DAD! DAD!!!" yelled Bobby again.

"Here I am Bobby," answered Dad.

Boy, was he ever glad to see his dad. He had been lost in the woods once before and he never again wanted that to happen.

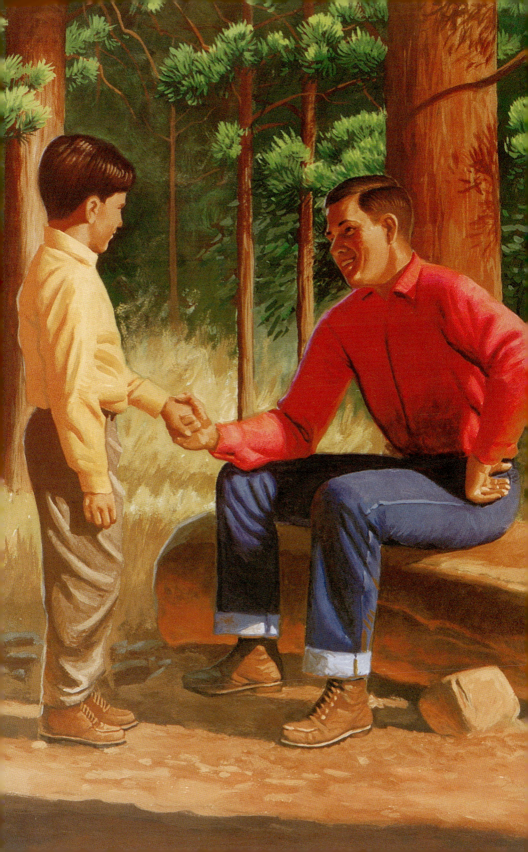

His dad was sitting on a nice flat rock beside the trail.... THE TRAIL!!! There it was.

He had been so busy climbing over the rocks and being the leader that he completely missed it.

He had headed off in another direction from the trail altogether and must have been trying to make his own trail.

He sat down beside his dad. It took some time to catch his breath.

Boy, had he been scared. He almost fell off the mountain.

It was hard being the leader. What a leader he was!

His dad put his arm around him and showed him the beautiful view again. Bobby caught his breath and when he could talk, the first thing he said was, "Dad, I'm sorry. I didn't mean to..." But before he could finish, his dad said, "That's all right, I understand. Bobby, didn't you notice that as we began this hike, you missed all the beautiful things I wanted to show you? You also kept your face to the ground looking for my footsteps. You bumped into me! We couldn't talk because you were so far

behind! Didn't you notice that after lunch when we walked together, you didn't have to look at the trail, because I was watching it for you?

"Didn't you notice that walking together, we saw deer and clouds? We were also able to talk about granddad and Heaven and all that neat stuff!" his dad continued.

"I kept the branches away and helped you over the high rocks and fallen trees," Dad said.

"Then, you got ahead of me. You picked the wrong trail. You had to duck the branches again and climb over the logs and rocks alone," said Bobby's dad. "You began to watch the ground instead of the beauty around you. And finally, you got so far ahead of me that you nearly fell off the mountain!" exclaimed his dad.

"You were so far away, we couldn't enjoy the walk together, Bobby," said his dad.

Bobby began to remember the lesson from Sunday School last Sunday. His teacher had told him that God loved us so much that He wants us to walk with Him all the time.

That God wants to be our friend and talk with us.

That He wants to protect us from all the dangers around us. We must stay close to Him so that He can help us.

On the way down the mountain that afternoon, Bobby thought of all that had happened. He thought of the way he had gotten so far behind that his dad couldn't help him. And how that was like God wanting to help us over the rough spots in our lives.

He thought of the branches that God wants to lift for us. He thought about the beautiful parts of this world that He placed here for

us to enjoy. He thought about how we miss these things, because we are so busy trying to get somewhere that we don't take time to look around.

He also understood, all of a sudden, that it was important not to get ahead of God. We lose sight of Him and can get into danger taking our own trail.

Bobby thought of the best time when he and his dad walked along side each other and talked. They laughed and saw all the beauty.

He understood that God wants us to walk alongside Him and talk with Him. God doesn't want us to be so busy that we miss His friendship.

On the way down the mountain that day, Bobby promised God that He would always walk alongside and always try to see the wonderful things that God has made.

Bobby thanked God for being his friend and for protecting him from dangers that he didn't even see.

Bobby walked close to his dad. They enjoyed watching the deer and squirrels. They laughed and talked all the way back to the car.

My steps have held to your paths; my feet have not slipped. Psalm 17:5

When you walk, your steps will not be hampered; when you run, you will not stumble. Proverb 4:12

In his heart, a man plans his course, but the LORD determines his steps. Proverb 16:9